P9-CQV-652

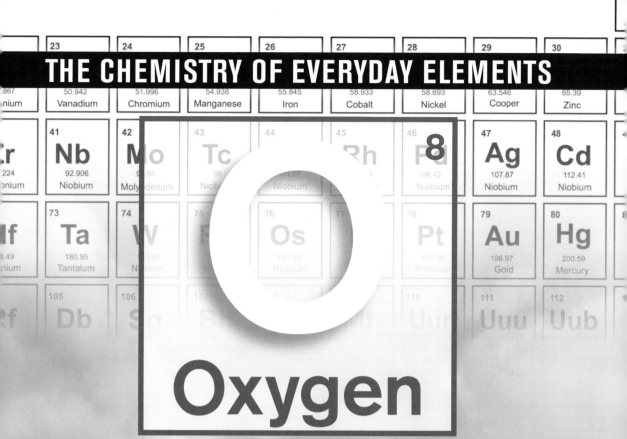

THE CHEMISTRY OF EVERYDAY ELEMENTS

O

8

Oxygen

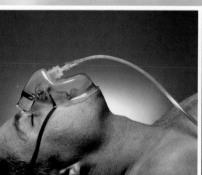

Mason Crest

THE CHEMISTRY OF EVERYDAY ELEMENTS

8

O

Oxygen

By Mari Rich

Mason Crest
450 Parkway Drive, Suite D
Broomall, PA 19008
www.masoncrest.com

Printed and bound in the United States of America.

Series ISBN: 978-1-4222-3837-0
Hardback ISBN: 978-1-4222-3843-1
EBook ISBN: 978-1-4222-7948-9

First printing
1 3 5 7 9 8 6 4 2

Produced by Shoreline Publishing Group LLC
Santa Barbara, California
Editorial Director: James Buckley Jr.
Designer: Patty Kelley
www.shorelinepublishing.com

Library of Congress Cataloging-in-Publication Data on file with the Publisher.

Cover photographs by Dreamstime.com: leeloommultipass (bkgd); 06photo (torch); itmejust (oxygen mask); infocus (leaves).

QR Codes disclaimer:

Oxygen

KEY ICONS TO LOOK FOR

 Words to Understand: These words with their easy-to-understand definitions will increase the reader's understanding of the text, while building vocabulary skills.

 Sidebars: This boxed material within the main text allows readers to build knowledge, gain insights, explore possibilities, and broaden their perspectives by weaving together additional information to provide realistic and holistic perspectives.

 Educational Videos: Readers can view videos by scanning our QR codes, providing them with additional educational content to supplement the text. Examples include news coverage, moments in history, speeches, iconic moments, and much more!

 Text-Dependent Questions: These questions send the reader back to the text for more careful attention to the evidence presented here.

 Research Projects: Readers are pointed toward areas of further inquiry connected to each chapter. Suggestions are provided for projects that encourage deeper research and analysis.

 Series Glossary of Key Terms: This back-of-the-book glossary contains terminology used throughout this series. Words found here increase the reader's ability to read and comprehend higher-level books and articles in this field.

Introduction

Have you felt a breeze on your face today? Drank a nice, cool glass of water? Lit a sturdy match and watched the glow of a campfire? All of those things—the solids, liquids, and gases around you—are composed of elements of the periodic table.

The periodic table is an arrangement of all the naturally occurring, and manufactured, elements known to humans at this point in time. An element is a substance that cannot be broken down into other, separate, substances. There are 92 elements that can be found naturally on Earth and in space. The remain-

---

WORDS TO UNDERSTAND

isotope   an atom of a specific element that has a different number of neutrons; it has the same atomic number but a different atomic mass

---

Don't hold your breath too long! We can't live without oxygen from the air.

ing 26 (and counting) have been manufactured and analyzed in a laboratory setting. These elements, alone or in combination with others, form and shape all the matter around us. From the air we breathe, to the water we drink, to the food we eat—all these things are made of elements.

We can learn a lot about an element just by finding its location on the periodic table. The periodic table has undergone several updates and reorganizations since it was first developed in 1869, until it became the modern version of the table used today. The periodic table is arranged into rows and columns by increasing atomic number. Each element has a unique atomic number. It is the number of protons in the nucleus of the atom. (All samples of an element have the same number of protons, but they may have a different number of neutrons in the nucleus. Atoms with the same number of protons but different number of neutrons are called **isotopes**.)

Each element on the periodic table is unique, having its own chemical and physical properties. Certain chemical properties can be

O 8

Oxygen

interpreted based on which group or row an element is placed. The periodic table also gives important information such as the number of protons and neutrons in the nucleus of one atom of an element, the number of electrons that surround the nucleus, the atomic mass, and the general size of the atom. It is also possible to predict which state of matter (gas, solid, or liquid) an element is designated by a chemical symbol—the letters that represent the element. The periodic table is a very useful tool as one begins to investigate chemistry and science in general. (For lots more on the periodic table, read *Understanding the Periodic Table*, another book in this series.)

This book is about the element oxygen. Oxygen, one of the most abundant elements in the universe, has eight protons and eight neutrons in its nucleus. A stable atom of oxygen has eight electrons. Oxygen is a gas under standard conditions.

How is oxygen a part of our lives? The most obvious answer is that we breathe it in every moment of the day; oxygen accounts for about 20 percent of the air around us. Along with hydrogen, it makes up the water we drink. Oxygen is vital to the process of photosynthesis, which allows plants to grow. You could say that without oxygen, life on Earth as we know it would cease to exist!

Periodic Table

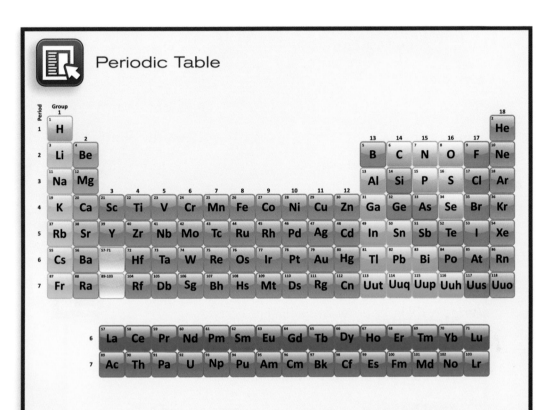

The Periodic Table of the Elements is arranged in numerical order. The number of each element is determined by the number of protons in its nucleus. The horizontal rows are called periods. The number of the elements increases across a period, from left to right. The vertical columns are called groups. Groups of elements share similar characteristics. The colors, which can vary depending on the way the creators design their version of the chart, also create related collections of elements, such as noble gases, metals, or nonmetals among others.

O
8
Oxygen

WORDS TO UNDERSTAND

alchemist   a person who practiced a science that was used in the Middle Ages with the goal of transforming ordinary metals into gold

apothecary   someone who prepares and sells medicines and drugs

combustion   a chemical reaction that occurs when oxygen combines with other substances to produce heat and light

respiration   the process of a living being taking in air in order to live

Discovery and History

W hile elements like gold, silver, copper, lead, and mercury had been known to man since antiquity, the first formal scientific discovery of an element did not occur until 1669, when Hennig Brand, a German **alchemist**, isolated and identified phosphorus during a process that required boiling 1,500 gallons of human urine that he had somehow stockpiled. (He had originally set out to discover the philosopher's stone, a legendary object that was said to be capable of turning base metals into gold.)

Oxygen also had to be "discovered." Well before it was isolated and identified, the idea of oxygen intrigued the scientific community. In the late 1500s, the famed Italian artist and scientist Leonardo da Vinci hypothesized that because air is not

Oxygen

entirely consumed when something is burned in it, it must consist of two distinct parts: one that is used up during the burning and one that is not. In 1608, a Dutch inventor Cornelis Drebbel found that potassium nitrate, when heated, released an unidentified gas. (Potassium nitrate is sometimes called saltpeter, and throughout history has been used for fertilizer, food preservation, manufacturing gunpowder and explosives, and a variety of other purposes.) Later, in 1668, British physician and chemist John Mayow suggested that air contained a gas he called "nitroarial spirit," which was consumed during breathing and burning—thus giving a fairly good description of oxygen without knowing it.

By the mid-18th century, scientists had embraced the concept of elements. Their goal was to break down Earth, air, fire, and water into more elemental components. During this period, they

Dutch inventor Cornelis Drebbel

were especially interested in the properties of air, because steam engines were then revolutionizing transportation, and the phenomenon of **combustion** was vitally important to that field.

Early Discoveries

The story of oxygen's discovery is marked by some con-

Joseph Priestley moved to America to support the Revolution there.

fusion and controversy. When science historians recount the tale, they mention three men—Joseph Priestley (1733–1804), Carl W. Scheele (1742–1786), and Antoine Lavoisier (1743–1794). Each of these men is usually given some level of credit.

In about 1772, Scheele, a Swedish **apothecary**, found that several compounds, including silver carbonate and potassium nitrate, all gave off the same gas when heated. An excited Scheele called the mystery gas "fire air," because it produced sparks when it came into contact with charcoal dust. Proving it never pays to procrastinate,

O ⁸

Oxygen

Scheele did not publish his findings, in a volume titled *Chemical Observations and Experiments on Air and Fire*, until 1777.

That delay allowed Priestley, a Unitarian clergyman and self-trained chemist from Great Britain, to steal much of Scheele's thunder. In 1775—a full two years before Scheele's publication—Priestley published his own findings in the second volume of his six-volume masterwork, *Experiments and Observations on Different Kinds of Air*. Priestley described a series of experiments he undertook in an attempt to un-

A statue to honor Swedish scientist Carl Scheele.

derstand the properties of different "airs," as gases were then known. Like other chemists of the day, he employed an inverted bell-shaped container on a raised platform. The bell captured the gases produced by experiments set up on a work surface below.

Priestley, who was then working as a live-in tutor and librarian for a wealthy patron, the Earl of Shelburne, discovered that a mouse placed in a sealed container would die. Furthermore, if a flame was placed in the container it would quickly go out. If, however, he placed a green plant in the container, the flame burned, and the mouse was able to breathe. Priestley stated that the plant was freshening the air in some way. (Because of this observation, Priestley is generally said to be the first to recognize the process of photosynthesis, whereby plants release oxygen into the air. To learn more about oxygen's importance to plants, see Chapter 4.)

On August 1, 1774, Priestley used a glass lens to focus sunlight on a lump of mercuric oxide in a sealed glass container. The gas that was produced caused a candle to burn with increased intensity and even had the ability to reignite a glowing ember. Additionally, when a mouse was placed in the container, it remained conscious for a full

Oxygen

hour, rather than the 15 minutes it would have taken to expire in a sealed container with the same quantity of common air. (Much to Priestley's surprise, once removed from the container, the seemingly dead mouse revived relatively quickly.) Emboldened, he breathed in the gas himself. "The feeling of it in my lungs was not sensibly different from that of common air, but I fancied that my breast felt peculiarly light and easy for some time afterwards," he wrote. "Who can tell but that in time, this pure air may become a fashionable article in luxury? Hitherto only two mice and myself have had the privilege of breathing it."

A Fateful Meeting

Soon after completing those experiments, Priestley accompanied the Earl of Shelburne on a trip to France. There he met Antoine Lavoisier, a lawyer who had been interested in science since his student days. (In 1764, the year he had earned his license to practice law, he had also published his first scientific paper; he was elected to the French Academy of Sciences just five years later—well before he turned 30.)

Antoine Lavoisier was sometimes called the Father of Modern Chemistry.

At the time of his meeting with Priestley, Lavoisier had been conducting his own experiments. In 1772 he had discovered that when phosphorus and sulfur (two substances that burned very easily) were set alight, the resulting products were heavier. That is, those products weighed more than the original phosphorus and sulfur. Lavoisier hypothesized that the phosphorus and sulfur were combining with something in the air to produce additional acids, but he had no idea what that something might be. Upon hearing that Priestley had discovered a mysterious gas that supported combustion much more effectively than ordinary air, he realized that he might have found his answer.

Lavoisier coined the name oxygen, drawing upon the Greek words

oxys meaning "acid" and *genes* meaning "forming." Lavoisier ultimately discovered that oxygen made up about 20 percent of the air we breathe. He also discovered that oxygen was essential for both combustion and **respiration**.

While Lavoisier drew upon the work of other scientists in his

The compound zinc oxide produces a layer that protects skin from the sun's rays.

experiments with air, he is still considered an important and innovative
chemist. In the late 1770s, while conducting further experiments, he discovered that when mercury oxide is
heated, its weight decreases and that
the oxygen gas it releases has exactly

What is conservation of mass?

the same weight as the amount lost. That finding was the basis for
a concept now considered fundamental—the law of conservation of
mass, which states that matter is conserved in chemical reactions.
Lavoisier is also credited with proposing the now common method of
naming a compound in a way that reflects something about its chemical composition. (For example, zinc oxide is very obviously the result
of zinc reacting with oxygen.)

Despite a long list of accomplishments (that even included helping
to establish the metric system), Lavoisier was sent to the guillotine as
a traitor in 1794, during the French Revolution, because he had once
worked for a company that gathered taxes for the government.

Priestley, too, had his share of political troubles. Because he had

Priestly supported the ideals—if not the executions—of the French Revolution.

been a vocal supporter of both the American and French Revolutions—and because his theological views were becoming increasingly radical—an angry mob burned his home. In 1794, he was forced to leave his native England. He fled to America, where he carried on with his research, enjoyed a friendship with Thomas Jefferson, and lived out the rest of his life.

Scheele's life was, by comparison, far less dramatic. Still, before dying at the age of 43, he had isolated glycerin (a sweet compound from animal fats now used in food); identified the elements barium, molybdenum, and tungsten; discovered that charcoal could absorb gases; investigated the properties of chlorine; and described how sunlight could reduce silver salts to metallic silver—the basis for early photography. So while he didn't get full credit for "discovering" oxygen, he carved his name in the history books quite successfully.

 Text-Dependent Questions

1. Where was Joseph Priestley from?

2. What animal was used in oxygen experiments?

3. How did Antoine Lavoisier die?

Research Project

Read more about Joseph Priestley. Why did he get sole credit for so long for discovering oxygen? How did historians find out about the other scientists?

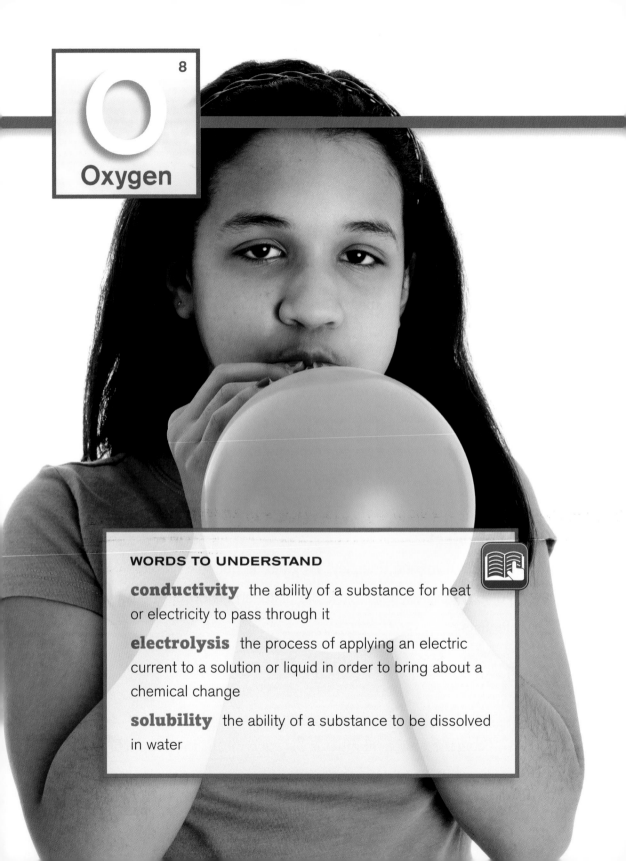

O 8

Oxygen

Chemical Properties

Oxygen, as Scheele, Priestley, and Lavoisier discovered, is an odorless, colorless, tasteless gaseous element. When today's scientists talk about the physical properties of an element, they go beyond simply describing its smell, color, and taste, though. They consider its **conductivity** (oxygen is a poor conductor of heat and electricity), its **solubility** (oxygen is slightly soluble in water, alcohol, and a few other liquids), and its density (1.429 grams per liter—denser than air).

By the Numbers

Oxygen's atomic number is 8, which means that it appears on the periodic table in the number 8 spot and identifies it as

Oxygen

8

having eight protons. The elements are placed on the table in the order of their atomic numbers, starting with the lowest—hydrogen at 1—and ending with the highest, ununoctium at 118. The last four elements to be added to the table were created in labs and accepted for

Liquid oxygen is so cold that it can freeze the outside of the pipes used to transport it through a factory using the substance in manufacturing.

inclusion in late 2015. Some scientists believe that no more elements can ever be created. Others say that the table is not yet complete and that new lab-created elements will continue to be made.

In their neutral state, atoms have an equal number of protons and electrons. Because an atom of oxygen has eight protons, it also has eight electrons; two of these orbit the nucleus in the inner shell of the atom, while six orbit an outer shell. That outermost orbital, however, actually has room for eight electrons, making it incomplete. That's one reason oxygen is known as the most reactive of all the non-metallic elements. Because of the available room on the outer orbital path, an oxygen atom can very easily react with other atoms and form bonds. (See Chapter 3 for more about how oxygen combines with other elements.)

Oxygen changes from a gas to a slightly bluish liquid at a temperature of −297.33°F (−182.96°C). A pool filled with liquid oxygen could be lovely to look at but would definitely be way too cold to swim in. At a temperature of −361.12°F (−218.4°C), liquid oxygen solidifies. A tiny, invisible oxygen molecule might sound like a fragile thing, but a 2012 study found that molecules of O_2 can survive pressures 19 million times higher than normal pressure of the air around it.

Oxygen

Oxygen as Ozone

An element's allotropes are different physical forms in which it can exist. (For example, graphite, charcoal, and diamond are all allotropes of carbon.) Oxygen's best-known allotrope is ozone. Ozone (written as O_3 to show three atoms bonded together) is pale blue in its gaseous form and has a distinctive smell. It was discovered in 1840, by the German chemist Christian Friedrich Schönbein, who was doing experiments on the **electrolysis** of water when he noticed an unusual odor. He derived the name for the new gas from the Greek word *ozein*, meaning "to smell."

Ozone is well known because it is often mentioned in news stories about climate change. However, it is actually relatively rare. There are only about three molecules of ozone for every 10 million air molecules. Still, ozone plays a vital role in the Earth's atmosphere, where it is found mostly in two regions. Some 90 percent is present in a layer known as the stratosphere, which begins about 10 miles

NASA: exploring ozone

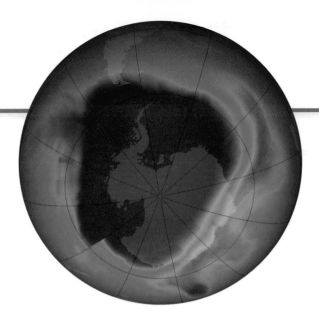

The colors in this image represent types of gas in the atmosphere. The purple indicates the "hole" in the layer of ozone surrounding the Earth.

or so above the Earth's surface and extends up for approximately 20 miles above that. The remaining ozone is found in the troposphere, a wide band of atmosphere below the stratosphere.

Ozone in the stratosphere is concentrated in a region referred to as the ozone layer, and it absorbs most of the damaging ultraviolet rays of the sun. That means only a small amount of that radiation reaches the Earth's surface. Without the filter provided by the ozone layer, more of the sun's ultraviolet radiation would reach the Earth's surface. That could spell great danger for all living things. In fact, scientists have recorded a dangerous reduction of the ozone layer, particularly above the Antarctic. They discovered that the ozone there was being destroyed by man-made chemicals called chlorofluorocarbons (CFCs), which are found mainly in spray aerosols. Laws have

O 8

Oxygen

been passed to ban many uses of CFCs. Thanks to that, the ozone layer shrinkage has slowed and is even coming back in some places.

Although the ozone in the lower atmosphere is chemically identical to that in the ozone layer, it is considered to be a pollutant in the

Polluted air, partly caused by ozone, can be harmful to people and animals. This image of Shanghai, China, clearly shows the effect of fossil fuel emissions.

troposphere. High levels of ozone can be toxic and can harm crops, forests, and even human health. Ozone near the surface is a key ingredient in the smog that blankets some cities.

 ## Text-Dependent Questions

1. What is oxygen's atomic number?

2. What role does ozone play in climate change?

3. The banning of what chemical has helped reduce ozone loss?

Research Project

Look into the "hole" in the ozone. Find out where it can most easily be seen. Locate images online that show how the size and shape of the hole changes through the year.

Oxygen and You

Oxygen is absolutely essential for sustaining life on Earth. It's in the air that we breathe and the water we drink, and it's a vital part of our bodies. In fact, every major class of molecule in our bodies—including proteins, carbohydrates, and fats—contains oxygen.

WORDS TO UNDERSTAND

cannula a thin tube inserted into a vein or body opening to administer medicine or to drain off fluid

debunk prove to be totally untrue

diaphragm a large muscle that separates the chest cavity from the stomach area

emphysema a disease of the lungs in which fluid builds up and prevents good breathing

tinnitus a condition in which ringing or buzzing is perceived in the ears

Because the mass of the human body is more than half water (H_2O), oxygen accounts for about 65 percent of our weight. The only other element that even comes close is carbon, which makes up about 18 percent. (What about calcium in our teeth and bones? You might think we have a lot, but calcium makes up only about 1.5 percent of us!)

Every Breath You Take

While non-scientists generally think of inhaling and exhaling air as simply "breathing," scientists refer to "respiration." That means the whole chain of processes that begins with inhaling and results in the air's oxygen being used in the cells of the body.

When we inhale, we draw air in through our noses or mouths. In our chest, our **diaphragm** lowers, the volume of our chest cavities expands, and the air flows into our lungs through the bronchial passages. Once there, the air's gases are exchanged between the lungs and the bloodstream in small air sacs called *alveoli*. (Our lungs contain almost 1,500 miles/2,414 km of airways and more than 300 million alveoli.)

Almost all the oxygen in the inhaled air is carried through the blood by attaching itself to hemoglobin. That's a protein in red blood cells. From there, the oxygen travels to the cells of the body. Each part of the body uses oxygen in different ways, such as breaking down glucose from sugar for energy. If we think of the blood as a transportation system, it's not just one-way. The bloodstream also whisks away waste products, such as carbon dioxide, which our cells have produced but have no use for. (Blood-carrying oxygen is bright red, while the blood returning carbon dioxide and other waste to our lungs is a purplish color.) Finally, we get rid of the carbon dioxide when we exhale.

Healthy adult humans breathe in and out about 15 to 20 times a minute, taking in some 13 pints of air in that time. We inhale more than 6 billion tons (5.4 billion metric tons) of oxygen each year. Not every part of the body that needs oxygen gets it from the bloodstream. For instance, the cornea—the transparent layer that forms the front of the eye—has no blood vessels. Oxygen goes directly into the cornea from the air.

The Air Up There

The air we breathe is not made up of pure oxygen: remember that Lavoisier discovered that oxygen made up only about 20 percent of the air. It's an unquestionably important part, but nitrogen, another common gas, is by far the most plentiful. Nitrogen makes up 78 percent of the air, oxygen 21 percent. In addition to oxygen and nitrogen, air also contains other gases, such as argon, helium, and methane. (Air also contains solids such as dust, pollen, microbes, and plant spores.) The level of air pressure differs from place to place, however. It's the highest at sea level, and it gets lower at high elevations.

A member of an Everest climbing team shows the bottles of oxygen that such climbers need to have with them at high altitude.

Reduced pressure makes it harder to breathe. That's why climbers trying to scale peaks like Mount Everest often carry extra oxygen with them. Everest's base camp on the Khumbu Glacier, in northeastern Nepal, is at an altitude of 17,600 feet (2,316 m). There, oxygen levels are just half of those found at sea level. That drops to one-third at the mountain's summit, which reaches almost 30,000 feet (9,144 m) above sea level.

The lowest levels of oxygen ever recorded in human blood were measured in 2009, in climbers who were nearing

Too Much Oxygen?

While too little oxygen is obviously dangerous, too much can also have bad effects. Breathing air with 80 percent oxygen for more than 12 hours can cause injury to the respiratory tract (lungs). That can lead to deadly fluid buildup. Having too much oxygen in the blood, which happens sometimes during spaceflight and scuba diving, for example, can result in **tinnitus**, nausea, irritability and confusion, and even seizures.

Everest's summit. Those test subjects had just a quarter of the normal amount of oxygen. Climbers are at risk of several oxygen-related health complications. Those include high-altitude pulmonary edema, a life-threatening condition in which fluid accumulates in the lungs. Shortly after a climber's brain starts to be deprived of oxygen, he or she can get dizzy, become extremely fatigued, and lose ability to make good decisions.

If the peak of a mountain sounds like a tough place to get oxygen, how about being in a sealed metal tube 40,000 feet (12,192 m) up in the air? That's you in an airplane, of course! But airplane passengers have little to fear. The cabins are pressurized, which means air at the right pressure is pumped in. In the very rare event an airline cabin loses pressure, the pilot will descend rapidly to an altitude of about 10,000 feet (3,048 m). At that level, the outside air has enough pressure for humans.

In a worst-case scenario, masks will drop from the ceiling. These are generally called oxygen masks, but airliners do not carry tanks of actual oxygen. The mask actually releases other chemical compounds that help passengers take in enough oxygen from the lower-pressure air. The pilot still has to get the plane to a safe altitude quickly.

Consider the case of an enclosed metal tube of an entirely different kind: a nuclear submarine, drifting 1,600 feet (488 m) under the sea. Engineers create breathable air for the sub's crew from sea water. They use machines that split the hydrogen and oxygen molecules of the ocean water with an electric current. That lets a submarine remain submerged for months at a time.

Oxygen and Medicine

Even on dry land and at sea level, of course, medical issues occur that require the use of extra oxygen. When doctors in the emergency room have to treat a patient suffering from severe injuries, one of the first steps they take is to make sure the airway

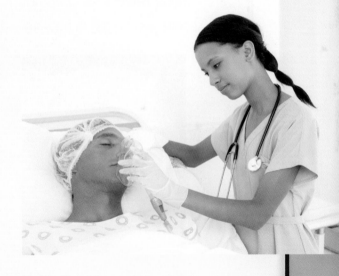

Masks like this provide nearly pure oxygen to patients in a hospital.

is clear. Then they give the patient compressed oxygen gas through a mask or nasal **cannula**. **Emphysema**, pulmonary disease, and other lung conditions can prevent the body from taking in and using oxygen. Those are now routinely treated—even at home—by inhaling oxygen from a small, portable tank.

Certain conditions are treated in hyperbaric chambers, a large machine in which the air pressure is increased to three times higher than normal. In these chambers, a patient's lungs can gather more oxygen than would normally be possible. As the blood carries the oxygen through the body, it fights bacteria and helps release useful substances like growth factors and stem cells, which aid in healing wounds and reducing infections.

Following time spent deep underwater, divers remain in a hyperbaric chamber to safely return to normal air pressure.

Oxygen Scams?

Some cities are now home to oxygen "bars." At such places, people pay by the minute to sniff O_2 scented with flavors like bayberry and peppermint. The bars are forbidden by the U.S. Food and Drug Administration (FDA) from saying that this is healthy or medical. However, the owners claim that a few minutes at the bar can make customers feel alert and relaxed, as well as free of headaches, hangovers, and sinus troubles. Experts warn that there are no long-term studies that prove that this type of oxygen therapy is beneficial to already healthy people.

Doctors also warn of another possible scam: supplements being marketed vitamin O or "liquid oxygen." That one is relatively easy to **debunk**. Oxygen can exist in a liquid form only at temperatures below −182.96°C! That hasn't stopped people from buying it in the hope that it will increase their energy, treat infections, or help with other ailments.

O 8

xygen

WORDS TO UNDERSTAND

ore   a naturally occurring solid material that contains a valuable component (such as a metal) that can be extracted by mining

radioactive isotope   form of the same chemical element with differing atomic mass whose nucleus is unstable; it let soff excess energy by spontaneously emitting radiation

Oxygen Combines

Remember that oxygen has only six electrons on its outermost shell? Those six electrons are essentially never transferred to another atom—oxygen may take in two electrons to fill that orbital but the original electrons aren't going to leave. Still, oxygen very easily reacts with almost all the other elements. Those combinations are a vital part of many parts of our lives.

Oxygen's Place at the Table

As with all elements, oxygen's placement on the periodic table gives strong clues about its properties. Oxygen appears at the top of column 6A or 16. That is directly over sulfur, selenium, tellurium, and polonium. The elements in that column

are said to belong to the chalcogen family. The name comes from a Greek word, *chalkos*, which means **ore**. (The first two members of the family, oxygen and sulfur, are found in almost all ores.) Polonium was in the news in 2006, when Alexander Litvinenko, a former Soviet KGB spy who had been granted asylum in the United Kingdom, fell mysteriously ill and died. Doctors discovered that he had been the victim of radiation poisoning. KGB agents had slipped him

Soviet critic Alexander Litvinenko was killed after being poisoned with polonium, a periodic table neighbor of oxygen.

Sulfur is a periodic table neighbor of oxygen, though seemingly quite different.

a lethal dose of polonium-201, a **radioactive isotope** of the element.

At first glance, it would seem unlikely that a harmless, odorless, colorless gas like oxygen could have anything in common with a metal like polonium. The elements in the chalcogen family all even look different from one another. Sulfur is a yellow solid, while selenium is black, for example. They differ in weight, as well, with the elements getting heavier as they appear further down the chart. Additionally, each of the chalcogens has a different melting point and boiling point. Some can conduct electricity, others can't. Despite all these differences, the chalcogens each have six electrons in their outermost shells, just like oxygen.

Going from left to right on the periodic table, the elements get more reactive. Because of their placement all the way over in column 16, oxygen and its fellow chalcogens are all highly reactive. There is, however, an exception to that general rule; column 18, all the way to the right, contains the *noble* gases: helium, neon, argon, krypton,

Oxygen 8 O

xenon, and radon. The name noble means that their outermost shells already have eight electrons and thus they don't "mingle" readily with other elements. There are also elements known as noble metals, such as gold, silver, and platinum, which resist chemical reactions. Because of this they do not corrode or oxidize—which makes them desirable as jewelry.

Oxidation

The primary way that oxygen combines with other elements is through oxidization. The word for this important process has two meanings. In one, it refers to the loss of at least one electron when two atoms interact. In another, it refers to the reaction that occurs when oxygen combines with a different element. In some cases, when oxygen and another element combine, it results in useful substances. For example, oxidation produces hydrogen peroxide (H_2O_2), which is used to clean wounds. In other cases, oxidation is not desir-

Watch an apple oxidize

able. It turns the edges of a cut apple brown and causes iron to rust. Sometimes *oxidize* and *rust* are even used to mean the same thing. It's important to remember, though, that not all metals that interact with oxygen disintegrate into rust. In the case of iron, oxidation causes the crispy brownish substance we call rust. Copper, however, forms a greenish coating called copper oxide.

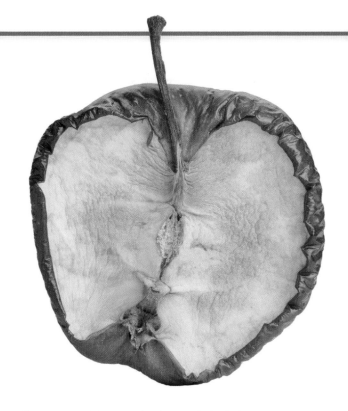

Oxygen combines with chemicals in fruit to turn exposed fruit brown.

The process of oxidation depends on the amount of oxygen present in the air and the chemical nature of the material it touches. It has to touch the substance, so having a barrier between the oxygen and the material helps prevent the process from starting. That's why fruit does not begin to turn brown until its protective skin is cut. That is also why car owners are advised to shield the paint on their vehicles

O ⁸
Oxygen

with a layer of wax. Oxidation can't occur if the oxygen can't reach a surface to combine with it.

In many cases, an element can form more than one oxide (the result of oxidation). Copper, for example, forms both the copper oxide mentioned above and cupric oxide. Nitrogen forms several oxides, including nitric oxide (NO), given as medicine to help blood vessels,

Hospitals use oxygen masks to make sure patients' blood is fully oxygenated.

and nitrous oxide (N_2O), sometimes used in dental procedures.

Two Hydrogen Atoms and an Oxygen Atom

Perhaps the most important of all the molecules containing oxygen is water, which even non-scientists often refer to as H_2O (h-two-oh).

This lake is filled with a compound of hydrogen and oxygen: water.

Water, as we can tell from its chemical name, is composed of two hydrogen (H) atoms and one oxygen (O) atom. The hydrogen atoms are bonded to the oxygen atom via a shared pair of electrons. Although the two elements are sharing electrons, it's not a totally fair split. The oxygen atom attracts electrons slightly more strongly than the hydrogen atoms. This unequal sharing gives the water molecule a slight negative charge near the oxygen atom and a slight positive charge near the hydrogen atoms.

Because of this, water is called a "polar" molecule. Water molecules attract each other because the positive end of one is strongly

Look closely and you'll see a bit of adhesion drawing the water up the glass sides.

attracted to the negative end of another. The bonds formed when this happens are known as hydrogen bonds, and they give water interesting physical properties. That special bond between the two elements also gives water the ability to create surface tension on liquids. The property of adhesion is the ability to stick to an unlike substance, such as when water slides up the surface of a glass.

Polarity also makes water a good solvent. That's because the hydrogen and oxygen atoms have a strong pull on other substances. Table salt, for example, is made from positive sodium ions bonded to negative chloride ions. Water easily dissolves salt because the positive side of the water molecules attracts the negative chloride ions. At the same time, the negative side of the water molecules attracts the positive sodium ions.

Oxygen and Combustion

You can't have fire without oxygen. Combustion is the name of any chemical reaction that includes rapid oxidation and the release of energy as heat and light. Fire is one form of combustion. When you start a campfire, start a car, heat your home, or strike a match, hydrocarbons react with oxygen to create fire. They also produce carbon dioxide and water vapor.

Most common fuels—including natural gas, propane, and wood—are made up of

Next time you roast marshmallows on a campfire, say thank you to oxygen for the assist!

The Chemistry of Everyday Elements

Hydrocarbons such as gasoline combine with oxygen and the fire from an engine's spark plug to create the power that drives combustion engines.

hydrocarbons. Many industrial systems use them because these re-actions release large amounts of heat. That heat can be used directly for warmth or converted into mechanical power. All three elements—fuel, oxygen, and heat source—must be present in order for combus-tion to take place. That's why even though gas and air may both be present in a fuel tank, it doesn't burst into flames because there is no source of heat in the tank.

Once combustion starts, however, the heat generated by the process itself will keep the process going. That's why, as long as it has enough oxygen, a fire will continue to burn.

 Text-Dependent Questions

1. What chemical was used to kill Alexander Litvenenko?

2. What does "noble" mean in chemistry?

3. What is needed for combustion?

Research Project

Combustion is more than just fire. Read about this scientific process and identify other forms of combustion. How is oxygen a vital part of some or all of them?

O

8

Oxygen

WORDS TO UNDERSTAND

dwarf star a star of average or low luminosity, mass, and size

organic compound a chemical compound in which one or more atoms of carbon are linked to atoms of other elements (most commonly hydrogen, oxygen, or nitrogen)

oxygenation a process that adds oxygen to a substance

Oxygen in Our World

Oxygen is the most abundant element in the Earth's crust—making up almost half of its weight. And because oxygen atoms are relatively large, the element makes up 96 percent of the crust's volume. Some geologists have even suggested (jokingly) that the crust is solid oxygen with just a few impurities scattered throughout. Oxygen also makes up 21 percent of our atmosphere and is found in water, many rocks and minerals, and various **organic compounds**. Ninety percent of the weight of the water in the oceans is from oxygen. Scientists say that oxygen is the third most abundant element in the universe and in the solar system, right after hydrogen and helium.

Oxygen

Oxygen in the Air Today

Most scientists agree that oxygen began to accumulate in the atmosphere some 2.5 billion years ago. They point to an event called the Great **Oxygenation**—or, more dramatically, the Oxygen Catastrophe. To understand the big event, it is first necessary to know about cyanobacteria, a type of blue-green algae. Scientists consider this organism as the first to produce oxygen through the process of photosynthesis. Of course, that is the process through which plants convert sunlight and air into energy to live.

Researchers are divided as to what precipitated the Great Oxygenation. Many suggest that changes in the Earth's geology caused the oxygen produced by photosynthesis to remain in the atmosphere. Whatever the reason, no one disputes that the buildup of oxygen in the atmosphere was bad news. It was a disaster for primitive microbes that had been thriving without oxygen. As the oxygen content in the air grew, it became deadly to those microbes.

About two billion years ago, the levels of oxygen in the world began to dip again. While oxygen levels are just one factor in animal evolution, some researchers think that the amount of oxygen in our atmosphere rebounded and finally became fully sufficient for animal respiration some 1 billion to 500 million years ago. That's just about when animals and plants, including the first early animals that evolved into dinosaurs, first appeared.

There is still much to discover about the evolution of the modern animal and how changing oxygen levels affected it. One recent study showed that about 300 million years ago, oxygen made up 35 percent

Was a higher percentage of oxygen in the ancient air a reason for dinosaurs' size?

Oxygen

of the air instead of today's 21 percent. In that oxygen-rich air, giant insects thrived, including dragonflies with wingspans of more than two feet (0.6 m). It is undeniable, however, that all animal life—including human—requires oxygen to survive.

Even organisms that we don't think of as "breathing" in the conventional sense require oxygen. Fish, for example, take oxygen out of the water through their gills. They "breathe" with gills as other animals, including humans, use lungs. A body of water without oxygen, perhaps because of pollution, will no longer support fish. (Proving that there is an exception to every rule, marine biologists exploring deep-ocean trenches have discovered organisms that "breathe" not oxygen but on other gases coming out of underwater vents.)

Oxygen in Space?

While some researchers focus on studying oxygen's role on Earth, others are looking to the cosmos. Most of the elements that allow us to live, including oxygen, were created in stars. Oxygen forms in the core of stars, with the fusion of a carbon-12 nucleus and a helium-4 nucleus. Recently, technology has even allowed researchers to look

This dwarf star has an outer layer made almost entirely of oxygen.

deep into oxygen's nucleus and begin to understand its structure. This is an important development because gaining a window into this process in stars can help scientists piece together the puzzle of how the universe is organized.

Scientists already know that oxygen is an important component in the clouds of gas and dust that form in space. New stars and planets can develop from that interstellar material. One newly developed white **dwarf star**, in fact, has an outermost layer of 99.9 percent pure oxygen. That makes its atmosphere the most oxygen-rich in the entire known universe.

Oxygen = Power!

Oxygen-based combustion was the key to most of the great advances that came during the period known as the Industrial

O 8

Oxygen

Revolution (c. 1760–1840). Among the most important was the steam engine. In this engine, coal is burned. The chemical bonds between its elements (carbon, hydrogen, and oxygen) break. The energy is released in the form of heat that makes steam drive the engine. That led to steam trains, steamboats, and steam-powered factories. Without oxygen, no trains, no steamboats. (A bit of trivia from this time period: The old phrase "standing in the limelight" came from the lights on theater stages. Lime was added to hydrogen and oxygen to create a bright, burning light!)

Later engines burned other substances, such as gasoline. The same chemical processes happened, all possible because of

Before gas or electric engines, steam engines powered locomotives.

the oxygen in those substances.

Combustion is still a major force in many industrial processes. That's because in all oxidation reactions, oxygen releases energy. People continue to create ways to capture that energy and use it for power. Oxygen

Inside the ISS

is combined with acetylene (C_2H_2) to produce an intense flame used for welding. Streams of high-pressure oxygen are used to burn away impurities in pig iron in order to produce high-quality steel. More than half of the pure oxygen produced in the United States each year is used to make metal.

While making steel doesn't often catch the public eye, rockets certainly do! Rocket fuel can be made by combining hydrogen and oxygen in liquid form. The cargo on manned space missions includes large tanks of very cold oxygen, which are used to help astronauts breathe. The oxygen is also used in the fuel cells that generate electricity to help run the International Space Station (ISS) or spacecraft. As a bonus, the chemical product of the fuel cell is ordinary H_2O,

Oxygen

which the astronauts use for drinking and cooling.

NASA scientists are at the forefront of finding other oxygen uses that would have amazed early scientists such as Priestley, Scheele, and Lavoisier. For example, early space shuttles often returned to Earth with damage. The heavy concentration of atomic oxygen in low orbit was reacting poorly with material on the shuttle exterior. NASA designed a thin, flexible coating of silicon dioxide. Because this material was already oxidized, it did not react to the atomic oxygen, and the exteriors of the spaceships stopped eroding.

In the process of their experiments, the NASA scientists discovered a great deal about the behavior of atomic oxygen. It turned out that it removed organic materials better than other processes. Its powers could be used to clean and restore artwork, because it doesn't affect the inorganic pigments in the paints, to sterilize medical implants, and more.

The Greening of the Planet

Power through oxygen comes from changing from a high-energy state to a low-energy state. Perhaps oxygen's most important process,

A fresh-picked apple would not be possible without oxygen's vital contribution.

though, is the reverse of that, and one that affects the entire planet. Photosynthesis is the process by which plants, algae, and some bacteria use the sunlight, water, and air to create oxygen. The plants take in the carbon dioxide that humans can't use to breathe. The energy from the sunlight combines with molecules from the water to change the carbon dioxide to oxygen.

At the same time, the plants use the glucose created in this process for food. The plants then release oxygen back into the air. Without this life-giving process, animal life—yes, that includes humans!—on Earth might not be possible. The word *photosynthesis* combined from the Greek words *photo*, meaning "light," and *synthesis*, meaning "put together," can be expressed by a simple chemical equation:

Oxygen

$$6CO_2 + 6H_2O + \text{Light Energy} \rightarrow C_6H_{12}O_6 + 6O_2$$

In other words, six molecules of CO_2 (carbon dioxide) combine with six molecules of H_2O (water) using light energy. The result is a single carbohydrate molecule $C_6H_{12}O_6$ (glucose, or sugar), plus six molecules of breathable oxygen. From carbon dioxide come sugars that power the plant and oxygen that powers us. Photosynthesis is sometimes called the chemical process most important to life on Earth. Without it, not only would there be no plants, but the planet could not sustain life of any kind—including human. Some scientists believe that if photosynthesis didn't occur, all of the oxygen in the entire at-

Plants take in sunlight and air, use the food they need, and release the oxygen we need to survive. Thanks, plants!

mosphere would be depleted within several thousand years.

Protecting the plant life on Earth then becomes a matter of our sheer survival. Without oxygen, life would end. So the ongoing environmental movement and the need to combat climate change that affects plant life are literally a battle for our lives.

 ## Text-Dependent Questions

1. What happened 2.5 billion years ago that affected oxygen?

2. What combines with oxygen to create a flame for welding?

3. Name the process that plants use to turn oxygen and light into energy.

Research Project

Read about the International Space Station. Prepare a short report on how the astronauts who live on it get enough oxygen to breathe and how that is related to their having enough water to drink, too.

FIND OUT MORE

Books

Canfield, Donald E. *Oxygen: A Four Billion Year History.* Princeton, NJ: Princeton University Press, 2014.

One of the world's leading authorities on geochemistry, Earth history, and the early oceans covers oxygen's vast history, emphasizing its relationship to the evolution of life and the evolving chemistry of the Earth.

Jackson, Joe. *A World on Fire: A Heretic, an Aristocrat, and the Race to Discover Oxygen.* New York: Penguin Books, 2014.

The author provides a detailed history of oxygen's discovery and the lives of the men involved.

Lane, Nick. *Oxygen: The Molecule That Made the World.* New York: Oxford University Press, 2004.

This volume, written by a biochemist, takes the reader on a journey to unravel the unexpected ways in which oxygen spurred the evolution of life and death.

Websites

periodic.lanl.gov/8.shtml

This site from the Los Alamos National Laboratory contains useful basic information about oxygen and the other elements.

education.jlab.org/itselemental/ele008.html

The Thomas Jefferson National Accelerator Facility (Jefferson Lab) maintains this page of interesting information about oxygen and its importance to our world.

www.livescience.com/28738-oxygen.html

Live Science offers a window into the natural and technological world, including the elements.

SERIES GLOSSARY OF KEY TERMS

carbohydrates a group of organic compounds including sugars, starches, and fiber

conductivity the ability of a substance for heat or electricity to pass through it

inert unable to bond with other matter

ion an atom with an electrical charge due to the loss or gain of an electron

isotope an atom of a specific element that has a different number of neutrons; it has the same atomic number but a different mass

nuclear fission process by which a nucleus is split into smaller parts, releasing massive amounts of energy

nuclear fusion process by which two atomic nuclei combine to form a heavier element while releasing energy

organic compound a chemical compound in which one or more atoms of carbon are linked to atoms of other elements (most commonly hydrogen, oxygen, or nitrogen)

solubility the ability of a substance to dissolve in a liquid

spectrum the range of electromagnetic radiation with respect to its wavelength or frequency; can sometimes be observed by characteristic colors or light

8

Oxygen

INDEX

Photo Credits

Adobe Images: Zealnanet 7, Family Business 10, comodigit 18, Rob 22, Saritphoto 24, wusuowei 28, wavebreakmedia 35, edwardolive 37, pedphoto36pm 41, dmitrimaruta 44, gburba 45, Rawich Liwlucksaneey 46, Wirepic 47, Thananit 48, Elenarts 53, Ekaterina Pokrovsky 59, Sergii Mostoviy 60. AP Images: Binod Joshi 33, Alistair Fuller 40. Dreamstime: Mikhail Markovskiy 14, Epicstock 38, Shawn Hempel 43, Wenbin Yu 56. NASA: Goddard Center 27, 50, ESA 55. Wikimedia: C. Van Sichem 12, 13, 17, 20.

About the Author

Mari Rich was educated at Lehman College, part of the public City University of New York. As a writer and editor, she has had many years of experience in the fields of university communications and reference publishing, most notably with the highly regarded periodical *Current Biography*, aimed at high school and college readers. She also edited and wrote for *World Authors, Leaders of the Information Age*, and *Nobel Laureates*. Currently, she spends much of her time writing about engineers and engineering.